For Gaye

Farrar Straus Giroux Books for Young Readers
An imprint of Macmillan Publishing Group, LLC
120 Broadway, New York, NY 10271

Copyright © 2020 by Allan Drummond
All rights reserved
Color separations by Bright Arts (H.K.) Ltd.
Printed in China by Toppan Leefung Printing Ltd., Dongguan City, Guangdong Province
Designed by Jen Keenan and Eileen Gilshian
First edition, 2020
1 3 5 7 9 10 8 6 4 2

mackids.com

Library of Congress Cataloging-in-Publication Data

Names: Drummond, Allan, author.
Title: Solar story : how one community lives alongside the world's biggest
solar plant / Allan Drummond.
Description: First edition. | New York : Farrar Straus and Giroux Books for
Young Readers, 2020. | Audience: Ages 4-8 | Audience: Grades K-1 |
Summary: "A nonfiction picture book about the largest solar power plant
in the world"— Provided by publisher.
Identifiers: LCCN 2019047161 | ISBN 9780374308995 (hardcover)
Subjects: LCSH: Solar power plants—Morocco—Ouarzazate
(Province)—Juvenile literature.
Classification: LCC TK1545 .D78 2020 | DDC 621.31/244096466—dc23
LC record available at https://lccn.loc.gov/2019047161

Our books may be purchased in bulk for promotional, educational, or business use.
Please contact your local bookseller or Macmillan Corporate and
Premium Sales Department at (800) 221-7945 ext. 5442 or by email
at MacmillanSpecialMarkets@macmillan.com.

allan drummond

Solar

Story

*How One Community Lives Alongside
the World's Biggest Solar Plant*

Farrar Straus Giroux
New York

It's a long, hot, and dusty walk to school.
The sun shines down on us nearly every day.

Sun, and more sun. Sometimes it seems
like that's the only thing going on here.

We live in Morocco. Right there, in the top left-hand corner of the map of Africa.

The windows on my side of our classroom look out at the High Atlas mountains.

Sometimes a cool breeze blows in.

But on the other side, the Sahara desert begins. Nothing but millions of square miles of rocks, sand, and hot sunshine. All the way across northern Africa. The desert landscape around Ghassate, our home, has looked the same for a very long time.

Our teacher, Miss Abdellam, likes to talk about the big changes that are happening in our world. She also likes asking big questions.

Making electricity from sunshine!

We all know the answers to *those* big questions. Why? Well, up on the high ground, close to our village . . .

. . . the world's largest solar power plant is under construction.

For a few years we've seen big trucks coming and going.

Now there are new pylons and wires all over, sending electricity far away to where it's needed.

Around the plant, there are miles of high safety fences.

On the long, hot, dusty walk back from school we can just see, far away, men and cranes working on top of what will soon be the world's tallest solar tower.

Big changes *are* happening around us,
but at my home things are much the same.
We still have our five sheep.

And our two cows.

We still cook on an open fire.

And bake our own bread.

Here's Mr. Mule—Dad's transport!

What's going on, Dad?

So, if big changes are happening in the world, what is solar power actually doing for us?

The next day Miss Abdellam asks another one of her big questions.

Okay, class. Sustainability. What does that mean?

Being strong and independent?

Er, peace?

"Peace"?

Ha! Ha!

Some kids giggle at Nadia's answer.

Miss Abdellam laughs. "Good answers! You're all correct. But in *different* ways. Sustainability means many things. Tonight I want you all to think about sustainability and write something about it. But first, the field trip!"

Our village is hidden away down by a riverbed that flows only in the winter.

Most of the year it's dry. There's hardly any water here.

We can grow just a few things . . . palms, almonds, crops to feed the animals.

MOROCCO

Morocco is a country in the northwest of the huge continent of Africa. It has many mountains and hundreds of miles of coastline. On the Atlantic side of Morocco's High Atlas mountain range there are lots of cities, plenty of farms, and all kinds of industry. But on the side nearest the Sahara desert, the landscape is much more arid because of lack of rain and the powerful desert sun.

By putting that sunlight to use, some scientists and engineers think the Sahara desert could become a very important supplier of solar energy not just to African countries, but to other countries as well. The Moroccan Agency for Sustainable Energy has taken a big step forward in making this vision a reality by deciding to build the largest concentrated solar power plant in the world right next to the Sahara desert.

Moroccan people have their origins in Arab countries and in African countries south of the Sahara desert. The Berber people, who have lived all over North Africa for thousands of years, also make up a large part of Morocco's population. In addition, Spanish, French, and Arab cultures have influenced Moroccan society and history, and many of its people come from these cultures, too.

Ghassate, in the Ouarzazate Province, is a rural community of about 1,200 households. Like some other communities near the new plant, Ghassate has mainly a Berber population that is highly skilled at surviving and farming in hot, dry conditions.

At the top of the hill there *used* to be nothing but rocks and stones. Sometimes a lizard.

Wow! Big lizard!

And always the sun shining down on us.

Careful!

But now look! There's the huge solar tower.

Nearly finished!

We've got a new
bridge over the riverbed.

And a brand-new road.

Everything's amazing
up here now . . .
because just ahead is
the BIGGEST solar
power plant IN THE
WORLD.

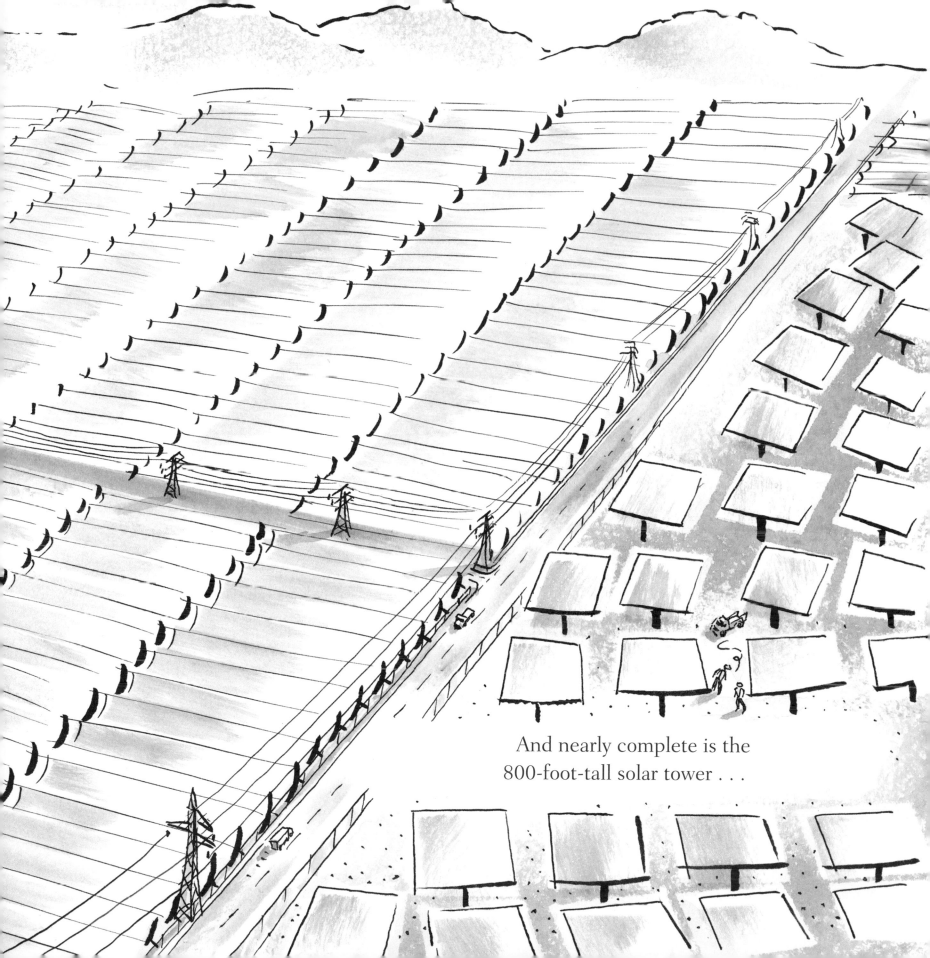

And nearly complete is the
800-foot-tall solar tower . . .

It's surrounded by thousands of mirrors, each the size of our classroom. They bounce the sun's rays onto the tower.

Cool! No. Hot!

"*Very* hot," says Miss Abdellam. "It will be one thousand degrees at the top, in fact."

The mirrors follow the sun as it moves across the sky.

THE NOOR SOLAR POWER PLANT

Most of the solar panels we see around us on buildings and in fields are fixed in place and face the general direction of the sun. They are usually black in color, and each panel converts the rays of the sun into electricity using the photovoltaic method, a chemical and physical process.

The Noor power plant in Morocco is very different. It is a *concentrated solar power plant*, consisting of four different parts. At Noor I and Noor II, thousands of huge mirrors are guided by computers to follow the sun as it crosses the sky from sunrise to sunset. The mirrors, placed in straight rows, are all curved in order to gather the sun's rays and *concentrate* them onto a glass tube that runs down all the rows for miles. This glass tube gets incredibly hot. It contains melted salt that is pumped around pipelines until reaching a water boiler where it creates steam that is used to turn machines called turbines to make electricity.

The solar tower at Noor III began operating in 2019. The rows of mirrors spread out in circles all around it. These mirrors also follow the sun and concentrate its rays onto the top part of the tower, heating pipes filled with melted salt. Again, the super-heated liquid is pumped to a water boiler that produces steam to power turbines that create electricity. At night, some of the molten salt is stored in insulated tanks and used to generate electricity during the hours when the sun is not shining.

Another part of the plant, Noor IV, will use fields of thousands of photovoltaic panels to produce electricity.

Like sunflowers!

You can see how the giant curved mirrors focus the hot sun onto a glass pipe.

As big as . . .

our bus!

Heat from this pipe and from the tower is used to make electricity.

At the center of the plant is the control room.

And at sunset the desert dust
is cleaned off the mirrors.

By using the sun we are not burning precious oil, coal, or gas. Here the sun shines on us nearly every day. *That's* sustainability!

Maybe one day, with the help of solar power, Morocco won't need to buy oil and coal from other countries to make electricity. *That's* energy independence. *And* it's sustainability!

But what *else* is sustainability? And what is the solar plant doing for us, right here, in our village? Well . . .

. . . there's Youssef's cousin Ahmed. When he helped build the plant, he learned how to weld metal. Now he's got his own workshop. He's independent—and he's given jobs to *two* people.

I want to learn to weld, too!

That's sustainability right there!

And the solar plant has started a new college in the nearby city. People go there by bus to learn new skills.

With wood,

with cloth,

with clay.

They hope to get jobs and start businesses themselves. And of course there will be new jobs at the solar plant.

That's sustainability.

SUSTAINABILITY

Solar power and wind power are both renewable sources of energy. They could also be called sustainable sources of energy because sunshine and wind are ever-present resources that won't run out from generation to generation.

Fossil fuels, like coal and oil, are not sustainable sources because they cannot be replaced once they have been burned. In the future, fuels like this will become more and more difficult to find. Coal and oil can also have harmful environmental effects that most scientists agree cannot be sustained.

The new solar plant at Noor has meant a big change for the local population. The Moroccan Agency for Sustainable Energy, which planned and built the solar power plant, knew that the power it produced would benefit the sustainability of Morocco's energy production. But they also knew that the plant would affect the farms, wildlife, businesses, leadership, and culture of the communities nearby.

The building of the plant has meant lots of new jobs. But once the plant is completed, many of these jobs will no longer exist. The sustainable idea here was to give people new skills that they could carry forward in their lives.

Morocco is growing in population and developing fast. Although the communities near the solar plant are remote, it is expected that with better roads, better water management, better farms, and more people with new skills, the area around the solar plant will thrive.

And the solar plant pays for experts to show our farmers better ways to keep sheep. Now some have a lot more than just five sheep! And this will help everyone get through hard times. *That's* sustainability!

Other farmers are learning new ways to grow bigger, better almonds, palms, and olives during the dry summer. We'll be able to grow much more of our own food. *That's* sustainability!

Until recently, the solar plant used our precious water for cleaning the mirrors and for cooling. Now they use air pressure and electric power from the plant. *That's* sustainability.

We've got a new mobile medical center. It helps us all—including mothers and their babies—to stay healthy! More sustainability!

Good night, Nadia!

See you in the morning, Jasmine!

Miss Abdellam says we will eventually get the internet at school, which we really do need. Education! Even more sustainability!
So there *is* actually a lot happening here!

AUTHOR'S NOTE

I was excited to start a picture book about the very important subject of solar power. First I decided to find out where the biggest solar plant in the world was. I was surprised to find that it was not situated in a highly developed country like the United States, but in a remote part of Morocco. My surprise is evidence of my own cultural short-sightedness. If I have learned anything in my study of the Noor project and its impact on the surrounding communities, it's that solutions to our energy and sustainability challenges can be found everywhere and require a global perspective from the start.

The plant is so big that you can easily see it if you zoom in on an internet mapping site. When I arrived there by car in 2017, my first impression was that it looked very much like an airport in the desert—flat ground surrounded by miles of fences and the solar tower far away in the distance.

My trip was supported with research funds from Cambridge School of Art, Anglia Ruskin University, and my thanks go to all the colleagues and students there who share my love for picture books. Thanks also to everyone at MASEN (the Moroccan Agency for Sustainable Energy) and ACWA Power, who organized my trip around the Noor plant. They also organized visits to the college at Ouarzazate and to villages, schools, and farms near the solar plant. Thanks also to L'Association des Animateurs des Colonies Educatives d'Ouarzazate.

And finally, very special thanks go to the teachers and students at École Oum Raman in Ghassate. The school was tiny, but the students were learning about big changes happening in the world. As I stood in one classroom, I saw maps and pictures on the walls and the view outside the window. It was then I realized that this was where my story should begin.

BIBLIOGRAPHY

For more information, check out these sources:

Ceurstemont, Sandrine. "The Colossal African Solar Farm that Could Power Europe." BBC Future. November 29, 2016. bbc.com/future/story/20161129-the-colossal-african-solar-farm-that-could-power-europe.

Parke, Phoebe and Chris Giles. "Morocco's Megawatt Solar Plant Powers Up." CNN. Updated May 17, 2018. cnn.com/2016/02/08/africa/ouarzazate-morocco-solar-plant/index.html.

Summers, Justine. "5 Largest Solar Farms in the World." Origin Energy. October 24, 2018. originenergy.com.au/blog/lifestyle/5-largest-solar-farms-in-the-world.html.

It's still a long, hot, and dusty walk to and from school, and the sun does shine on us nearly every day. But that's not the only thing that's going on here.

Living alongside the world's largest solar plant means we've all started thinking about the future . . .

. . . not just the future of our community. Or the future of Morocco. Or the future of Africa. Sustainability is a way of thinking about the future of the whole world!

Maybe, because so many wars are about oil and other resources, sustainability will lead to a more peaceful world.

Maybe Nadia is right! Maybe sustainability *could* mean peace!